Music Minus One Drummer

Set List – Volume 2

WEEKEND WARRIORS

LADIES NIGHT

mmo

7162

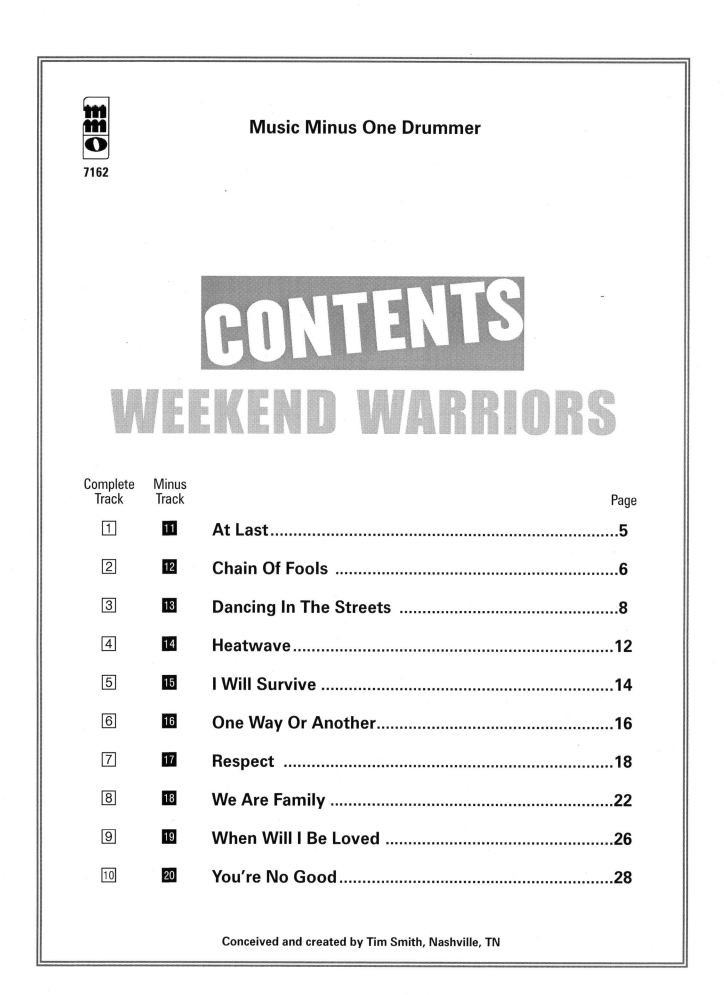

Music Minus One Drummer

7162

CONTENTS
WEEKEND WARRIORS

Conceived and created by Tim Smith, Nashville, TN

ISBN 1-59615-863-4

At Last

Sometimes a great song and great performance simply create magic. Such is the case with Etta James' version of "At Last." The song was written for a musical film, "Orchestra Wives" in 1941 and was subsequently performed by several bands of the Big Band Era. Then in 1960, Etta James recorded it as part of her debut album "At Last!" on Chess records. Though the song peaked at number 2 on the R&B charts, it only reached number 47 on the Billboard Hot 100.

Somehow, however, the magic of that recording continues to influence people, and as a result, "At Last" is one of the most requested songs you will need to learn in order to play weddings and anniversary parties. The song has the basic R&B, blues 12/8 feel. It can be played with brushes in both hands or with a stick in the right hand and a brush in the left. (If you are a "lefty," just reverse that!) This is so a more definitive hi-hat and ride cymbal part can be achieved. There is little or no bass drum on the original, but for modern day needs, we added bass drum. Here is the basic feel.

The bridge feel would be the same, only the ride cymbal would replace the hi-hat in the groove.

At Last

As Recorded By Etta James

Music by HARRY WARREN
Lyrics by MACK GORDON

12/8 Feel Throughout
♩ = 59

At last my true love has come along
My lonely days are over
And life is like a song

Oh yeah, yeah
At last the skies above are blue
My heart was wrapped up in clover
The night I looked at you

I found a dream that I could speak to
A dream that I could call my own
I found a thrill to press my cheek to
A thrill that I have never known

Oh yeah, yeah, you smile, you smile
Oh and then the spell was cast
And here we are in heaven
For you are mine...at last

Chain of Fools

As Recorded by Aretha Franklin

Words and Music by Don Covay

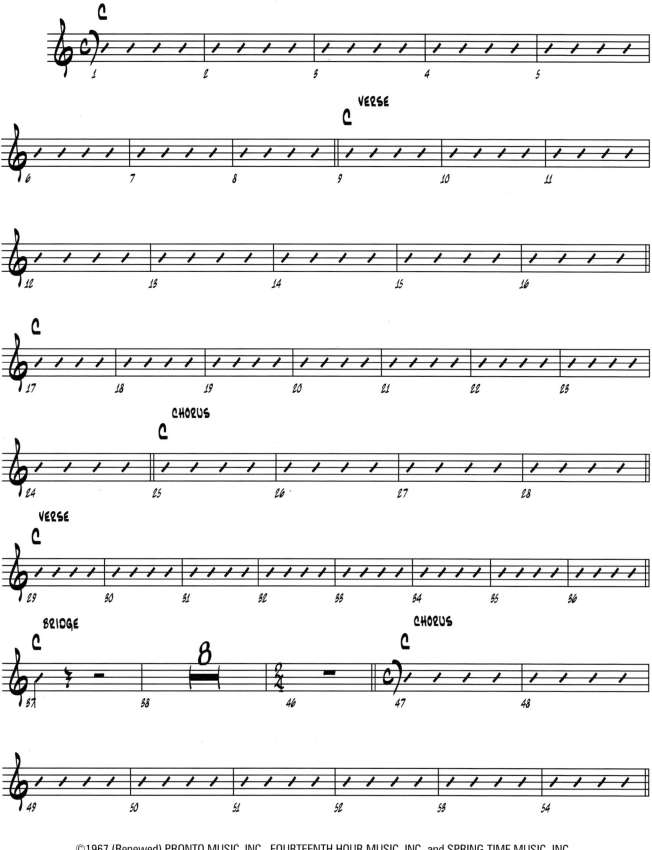

CHAIN OF FOOLS

VERSE

Bars 55, 56, 57, 58, 59, 60, 61

CHORUS

Bars 62, 63, 64, 65, 66

Bars 67, 68, 69, 70, 71

Chorus:
Chain, chain, chain
Chain, chain, chain
Chain, chain, chain, chain, chain, chain, chain
Chain of fools

For five long years
I thought that you were my man
But I found out
I'm just a link in your chain

You got me where you want me
I ain't nothin' but your fool
Ya treated me mean
Oh you treated me cruel.

Chain, chain, chain
Chain of fools

Every chain, has got a weak link
I might be weak yeah
But I'll give you strength
Oh hey

You told me to leave you alone
My father said "Come on home."
My doctor said "Take it easy"
Oh but your lovin' is much too strong
I'm added to your

Chorus

One of these mornings
The chain is gonna break
But up until the day
I'm gonna take all I can take, oh hey

Chorus
Chorus

Chain of Fools

Aretha Franklin's "Chain of Fools" is all about the feeling and attitude. The song, written by Don Covay, was released as a single in 1967. It reached the number 1 slot on the R&B chart and number 2 on the pop chart. The song is one of a very select few which features no chord change at all. In Aretha's version, the entire song is over one chord. This is a basic straight eighth note R&B groove. The bridge has a breakdown where the drummer plays bass drum on beats 2 and 4. Halfway through the third chorus, the right hand plays a classic Bernard Purdie ride cymbal "bell pattern. There are also some random hi-hat scoops (signature Purdie!) throughout. Here is the basic groove for the song.

Here is the ride bell pattern-the bell note on beat 2 and beat 4 is a ghost note and sometimes is not played at all.

Dancing in the Streets

As Recorded by Martha Reeves and the Vandellas

Words and Music by
Marvin Gaye, Ivy Hunter
and William Stevenson

MMO 7162

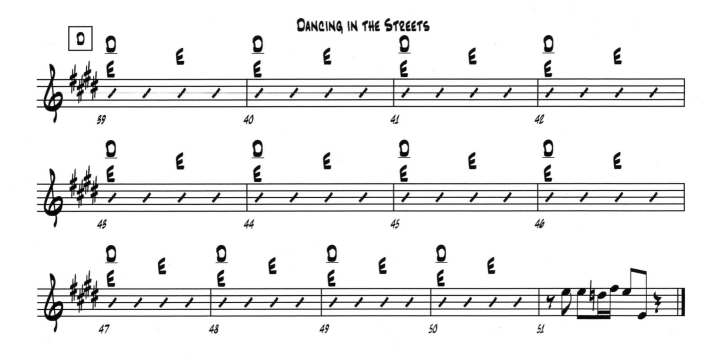

DANCING IN THE STREETS

Callin' out around the world
Are you ready for a brand new beat?
Summer's here and the time is right
For dancin' in the street.
They're dancin' in Chicago
Down in New Orleans
In New York City

Chorus

All we need is music
Sweet music
They'll be music everywhere
They'll be swingin' and swayin'
And records playin'
Dancin' in the street
Aw, it doesn't matter what you wear
Just as long as you are there
So come on every guy, grab a girl
Everywhere around the world

They'll be dancin'
They're dancin' in the street
This is an invitation across the nation
A chance for folks to meet
They'll be laughin', singin', and music swingin'
We're dancin' in the street.

Philadelphia, P.A.
Baltimore and D.C.
Can't forget the Motor City

Chorus

They're dancin', They're dancin' in the street.
Way down in L.A. everyday
They're dancin' in the street.
Let's form a big strong line
Get in time They're dancin' in the street
Dancin' in the street

Dancing in the Street

"Dancing in the Street" is one of those songs that proves the adage that a great song can be done different ways and styles and still be great. From its original version released by Martha and the Vandellas in 1964 to Van Halen's version in 1982, the song maintains its infectious feel and creates smiles. The song was written by future superstar Marvin Gaye (who also played drums on the track), William "Mickey" Stevenson and Ivy Jo Hunter. It was first recorded for Martha Reeves at the Hitsville Studios in Detroit. As with the other Motown hits of the period, this session consisted of the musicians known as The Funk Brothers. This is a classic straight eighth Motown groove. There is an occasional accent on "and" of beat 4. There is also a tambourine part that starts at measure 5. It is a simple 2 and 4 backbeat on top of the snare drum part. This could be covered by putting a "ching-ring" or hi-hat mounted tambourine on your hi-hat and playing the backbeats with your hi-hat foot. Here is the groove.

Enjoy playing this "Dancing in the Streets." Break this song out when you need the party to get going and you will be sure to have them dancing.

Heat Wave

What is not to like about Martha and the Vandellas' "Heat Wave"? Take an incredible shuffle beat, pair it with fantastic lyrics and vocal performances, and it is simply a hit. "Heat Wave" was re-leased as a single in July 1963 on the Gordy label, a subsidiary of the Motown label. The song WAS a hit, reaching number 4 on the Billboard Hot 100 and topping the R&B chart at number 1. The recording was done at the Hitsville Studio with the tracks being played by the legendary session players who worked there nicknamed The Funk Brothers. The guitar work was done by Robert White and Eddie Willis.

The Funk Brothers were recording virtually every day and even in 1963 they had become expert in finding parts that meshed together. Such is the case on "Heat Wave". This song is a classic shuffle groove. On the Motown track, it is played as a two hand shuffle with the right hand on the hi-hat. At the volume most drummers now have to play, it is easier to play this groove with the right hand playing the shuffle on the snare drum and the left hand playing the back beats only.

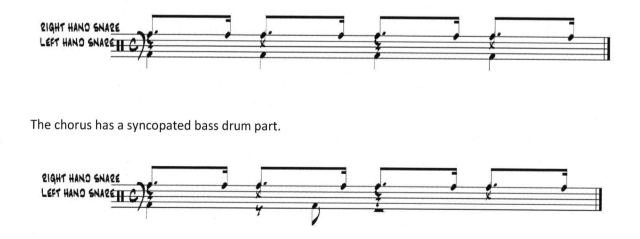

The chorus has a syncopated bass drum part.

There is a tambourine playing quarter notes from measure 5 to the end.

Heatwave

As Recorded by Martha Reeves and the Vandellas

Words and Music by
Edward Holland, Lamont Dozier
and Brian Holland

MMO 7162

Heatwave

Whenever I'm with him
Something inside
Starts to burning'
And I'm filled with desire
Could it be the devil in me
Or is this the way it's supposed to be

Chorus
Just like a heatwave
Burning in my heart
Can't keep from cryin'
It's tearing me apart.

Whenever he calls my name
So slow, sweet and plain
I feel, yeah, yeah, well I feel that burning flame
Has my blood pressure got a hold on me
Or is this the way love's supposed to be.

Chorus

Sometimes I stare in space
Tears all over my face
I can't explain it, don't understand it
I ain't never felt like this before
But that doesn't mean it has me amazed
I don't know what to do, my head's in a haze

Chorus

Yeah yeah, yeah yeah
Yeah, yeah
Yeah yeah, yeah yeah
Yeah, yeah, oh

But that doesn't mean it has me amazed
I don't know what to do, my head's in a haze
It's like a heatwave
Burnin in my heart.

I Will Survive

As Recorded By Gloria Gaynor

Words and Music by
Dino Fekaris and Frederick J. Perren

I Will Survive

At first I was afraid, I was petrified
Kept thinking I could never live without you by my side
But then I spent so many nights thinking how you did me wrong
And I grew strong and I learned how to get along

And so you're back from outer space
I just walked in to find you here with that sad look on your face
I should have changed that stupid lock
I should have made you leave your key
If I'd known for just one second you'd be back to bother me

Chorus
Go on now go, walk out the door, just turn around now
'Cause you're not welcome anymore
Weren't you the one who tried to hurt me with goodbye?
Did you think I'd crumble? Did you think I'd lay down and die.
Oh no not I, I will survive
Oh as long as I know how to love. I know I'll stay alive.
I've got all my life to live. I've got all my love to give.

And I'll survive, I will survive, hey, hey

It took all the strength I had not to fall apart
Kept trying hard to mend the pieces of my broken heart
And I spent oh so many nights just feeling sorry for myself
I used to cry, but now I hold my head up high

And you see me, somebody new
I'm not that chained up little person still in love with you
And so you felt like dropping in and just expect me to be free
But now I'm saving all my loving for someone who's loving me

Chorus

Chorus

One Way or Another

AS RECORDED BY BLONDIE

Words and Music by
Deborah Harry and Nigel Harrison

♩ = 162

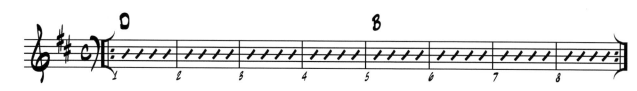

One Way or Another

One way or another I'm gonna find ya
I'm gonna getcha, getcha, getcha, getcha
One way or another I'm gonna win ya
I'm gonna getcha, getcha, getcha, getcha
One way or another I'm gonna see ya
I'm gonna meet ya, meet ya, meet ya, meet ya
One day, maybe next week, I'm gonna meet ya
I'm gonna meet ya, I'm meet ya

I will drive past your house
And if the lights are all out
I'll see who's around

One way or another I'm gonna find ya
I'm gonna getcha, getcha, getcha, getcha
One way or another I'm gonna win ya
I'll getcha, I'll getcha
One way or another I'm gonna see ya
I'm gonna meet ya, meet ya, meet ya, meet ya
One day, maybe next week, I'm gonna meet ya
I'll meet ya, yeah

And if the lights are all out
I'll follow your bus downtown
See who's hangin' out

One way or another I'm gonna lose ya
I'm gonna give you the slip
A slip of the hip or another, I'm gonna lose ya
I'm gonna trick ya, I'll trick ya

One way or another I'm gonna lose ya
I'm gonna trick ya, trick ya, trick ya, trick ya
One way or another I'm gonna lose ya
I'm gonna give you the slip

I'll walk down the mall, stand over by the wall
Where I can see it all, find out who you call
Lead you to the supermarket
Check out some specials and rat food, get lost in the crowd

One way or another I'm gonna getcha
I'll getcha, I'll getcha, getcha, getcha, getcha (Where I can see it all, find out who you call)
One way or another I'm gonna getcha
I'll getcha, I'll getcha, getcha, getcha, getcha (Where I can see it all, find out who you call)
One way or another I'm gonna getcha
I'll getcha, I'll getcha, getcha, getcha, getcha (Where I can see it all, find out who you call)
One way or another I'm gonna getcha
I'll getcha, I'll getcha, getcha, getcha, getcha(Where I can see it all, find out who you call)
One way or another I'm gonna getcha
I'll getcha, I'll getcha, getcha, getcha, getcha (Where I can see it all, find out who you call)
One way or another I'm gonna getcha
I'll getcha, I'll getcha, getcha, getcha, getcha (Where I can see it all, find out who you call)

Respect

As Recorded by Aretha Franklin

Words and Music
by Otis Redding

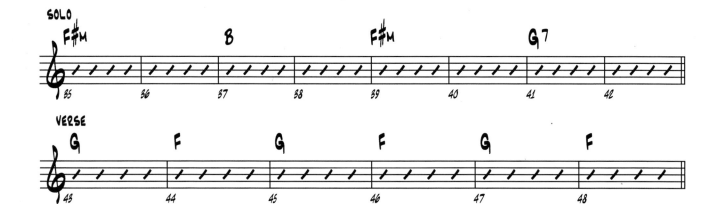

What you want
Baby, I got it
What you need
Do you know I got it
All I'm askin'
Is for a little respect when you come home
Baby when you get home
Yeah

I ain't gonna do you wrong, while you're gone
Ain't gonna do you wrong 'cause I don't want to.
All I'm askin'
Is for a little respect when you come home
Hey baby
When you get home
Mister

I'm about to give you all my money
And all I'm askin' in return honey
Is to give me my propers
When you get home
Yeah baby
When you get home
Yeah

Ooh your kisses
Sweeter than honey
And guess what baby
So is my money
All I want you to do for me
Is give it to me when you get home
Yeah baby
When you come home
Yeah

R-E-S-P-E-C-T
Find out what it means to me
R-E-S-P-E-C-T
Take care, TCB

Oh
A little respect
Whoa babe
A little respect
I get tired
Keep on tryin'
You're runnin' out of fools
And I ain't lyin'
Better give it to me
When you come
Or yl'll be walkin'
Out that door

I Will Survive

Let's just admit it: very few of us have no feelings about this song. Both as a disco phenomenon and an iconic "girl" song, "I Will Survive" is a classic. The drum work on the original recording is illustrative of the pop drum style of the disco era. Originally released as the "B" side of a completely forgotten song in 1978, the song cemented Gloria Gaynor's role as a major player in the history of disco. This song has the 16th note hi-hat with the "pea-soup" open and close part throughout. This is quintessential New York disco of the seventies.

There is a percussionist on this recording playing bongos throughout.

One Way or Another

Blondie released "One Way or Another" in 1978, and it rose up the charts to number 24 on Billboard's Hot 100. As part of the New Wave movement of the late 1970's it walked a delicate line between being too "pop" and too "punk." What the song created was a great feeling with a really tight rhythm groove and an almost theatrical vocal performance. As a package, the song was catchy with an aggressive attitude that still resonates today. This song has to be played with a 70's "punk" feel, loose, raucous, and lots of fun! Here are the major sections of the drum groove.

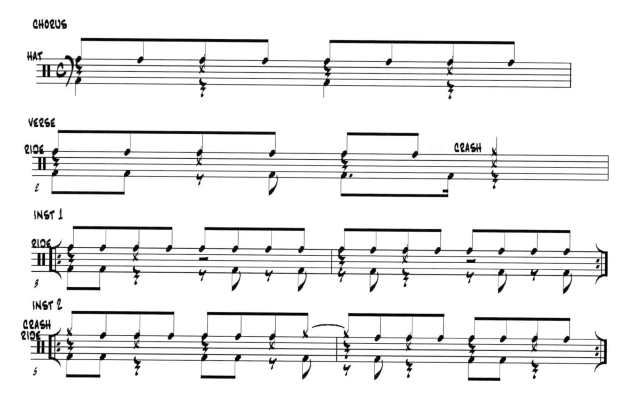

Respect

When it comes to songs that have endured, Aretha Franklin's "Respect" has to be near the top of the list. What is not as widely known is that Aretha's version was actually a cover of its original recorded in 1965 by its composer Otis Redding. The Aretha Franklin version was recorded on February 14, 1967 at Atlantic Records Studio in New York City with music icons Jerry Wexler and Arif Mardin producing. The song went on to top both the R&B and Pop charts and propelled Aretha Franklin into international stardom. This song uses the same R&B groove throughout. The "stop time" section has a 5 stroke roll into the downbeat of each stop.

MMO 7162

We Are Family

As Recorded by Sister Sledge

Words and Music by
Nile Rodgers and Bernard Edwards

WE ARE FAMILY

Chorus:
We are family
I got all my sisters with me
We are family
Get up ev'rybody sing

Ev'rybody can see we're together
As we walk on by
(Fly) and we fly just like birds of a feather
I tell no lie
(All) of the people around us they say
Can they be that close
Just let me state for the record
We're giving love a family dose.

Chorus
Chorus

Living life is fun and we've just begun
To get our share of the world's delights
(High) high hopes we have for the future
And our goal's in sight
(We) no we don't get depressed
Here's what we call our golden rule
Have faith in you and the things you do
You won't go wrong
This is our family jewel

Chorus
Chorus

We are Family

While Sister Sledge had other hits, they will always be identified by their 1979 smash hit song "We Are Family." The song, written by Nile Rodgers and Bernard Edwards of the band *Chic,* was pitched to Atlantic Records by Rodgers and Edwards, but Atlantic turned it down. Released on Cotillion Records, the song became a smash it, reaching number 2 on the pop chart and number 1 on the R&B chart.

This song has one of the classic R&B and disco grooves of the 70's. The bass drum is on 1 and 3 with an occasional 16th note grace note just prior to beat 3. The hi-hat is played with and "up-beat" feel accomplished by accenting the "and" of each beat. Here is the basic groove.

Here is the groove with the added bass drum grace note.

Music Minus One
DISTINGUISHED ACCOMPANIMENT EDITIONS

Drums

Chamber Classics
_____ STRAVINSKY L'Histoire du Soldat..MMO CD 5014 $29.98

Jazz, Standards and Big Band
_____ 2+2=5: A Study Odd Times ....MMO CD 2048 $19.98
_____ Drum Pad Stick Skin: Jazz play-alongs ....MMO CD 5006 $19.98
_____ Drum Star Jazz Combos ....MMO CD 5005 $19.98
_____ Eight Men in Search of a Drummer........................MMO CD 5010 $19.98
_____ For Drummers Only: Jazz Band Music ....MMO CD 5002 $19.98
_____ From Dixie to Swing ....MMO CD 5011 $19.98
_____ Funkdawgs: Jazz Fusion Unleashed ....MMO CD 2035 $19.98
_____ Isle of Orleans...MMO CD 5016 $19.98
_____ Jump, Jive and Wail: 6 Swing Bands ....MMO CD 5007 $19.98
_____ Modern Jazz Drumming ....MMO CD 5001 $19.98
_____ New Orleans Classics...MMO CD 5017 $19.98
_____ Northern Lights ....MMO CD 2008 $19.98
_____ Open Session: Greg Burrows Quintet ....MMO CD 5013 $19.98
_____ Studio Call: Film Scores ....MMO CD 2074 $19.98
_____ Studio Call: Pop/Country ....MMO CD 2099 $19.98
_____ Studio Call: Rock/Funk......................................MMO CD 2094 $19.98
_____ Studio Call: Top 40 'MOR' ....MMO CD 2064 $19.98
_____ Studio City ....MMO CD 2028 $19.98
_____ Take One (minus Drums) ....MMO CD 2018 $19.98
_____ Adventures in N.Y. & Chicago Jazz ....MMO CD 5008 $19.98

Rock 'n' Roll
_____ Fabulous Sounds of Rock Drums ....MMO CD 5012 $19.98
_____ Sit-in w/Jim Chapin ....MMO CD 5004 $19.98
_____ Weekend Warriors, vol. 1....................................MMO CD 7161 $19.98
_____ Wipe-Out ....MMO CD 5003 $19.98

Student Series
_____ Classical Percussion...MMO CD 5009 $34.98

All Prices Subject To Change

When Will I Be Loved

As Recorded By Linda Ronstadt

Words and Music by Phil Everly

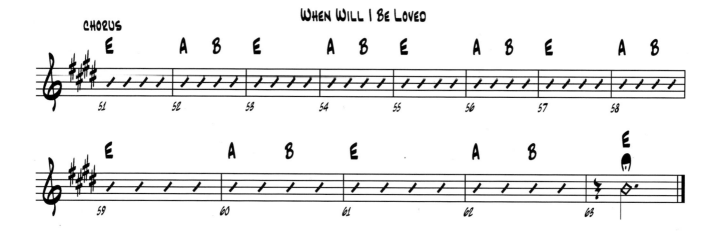

When Will I Be Loved

I've been cheated	I've been made blue
Been mistreated	I've been lied to
When will I be loved?	When will I be loved?
I've been put down	Bridge
I've been pushed 'round	
When will I be loved?	I've been cheated
	Been mistreated
Bridge	When will I be loved?
When I find a new man	Tell me, when will I be loved?
That I want for mine	
He always breaks my heart in two	
It happens every time	

When Will I Be Loved

On her Heart Like a Wheel album, Linda Ronstadt did covers on some amazing songs. From her number 1 hit "Your No Good" which is also in this book, to her cover of the Everly Brothers' "When Will I Be Loved", she and her producer Peter Asher crafted some of the very best new versions of songs that were recorded in the early '80's. At the core of that is the stellar "When Will I Be Loved" which is really a *tour de force* for multi-instrumentalist Andrew Gold. On the surface, the song is a simple track---bass, drums, and guitar. The drum track is a "rock style" shuffle. The chorus has the right hand playing the shuffle on the hi-hat. The verse has a simpler quarter note high hat part.

MMO 7162

28

You're No Good

AS RECORDED BY LINDA RONSTADT

Words and Music by
Clint Ballard, Jr.

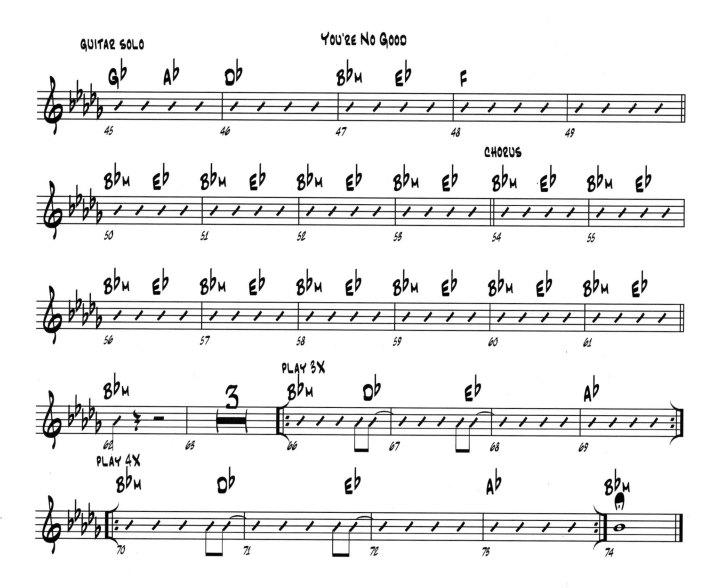

Feelin' better now that we're through	I broke a heart that's gentle and true
Feelin' better 'cause I'm over you	Well I broke a heart over someone like you
I learned my lesson, it left a scar	I'll beg his forgiveness on bended knee
Now I see how you really are	I wouldn't blame him if he said to me

Chorus	Chorus
You're no good	
You're no good	I'm tellin' you now baby
You're no good	And I'm going my way
Baby you're no good	Forget about you baby
I'm gonna say it again	'Cause I'm leavin' to stay
You're no good	
You're no good	Chorus
You're no good	
	Oh, no no
Baby you're no good	You're no good
	You're no good
	You're no good
	Baby you're no good

You're No Good

As a number 1 single for Linda Ronstadt from her Heart Like a Wheel album, "You're No Good" featured great production by Peter Asher and terrific keyboard and guitar work by Andrew Gold. The song, written by Clint Ballard, Jr., and first recorded in 1963, had such a great lyrical "hook" that Andrew Gold had the task of bringing the instrumental element of the song to life. From his original entrance in the intro, playing a simple rhythm part to his signature licks on the end, Gold's guitar work became as much a signature for the song as did Ronstadt's vocals. This song has a very sparse bass drum part throughout. When I heard Russ Kunkel playing this live with Linda Ronstadt, there was a busier bass drum. Here are the various grooves.

Weekend Warriors

LADIES NIGHT

For most of us, the true joy of music is sharing it. While there are millions of musicians *jamming* in their basements with headphones and an audience of the family pet, the true experience is walking into a venue and playing songs that put people on the dance floor or at least put a lot of smiles on their faces as they sing along. This series is a wonderful tool to help facilitate that, whether you are a teenager wanting to figure out how to make some gas money on weekends, to a working band that wants to actually capture the essence of the original hits – **Weekend Warriors** is for you. Whether you use this as an educational tool, a play along product, or a rehearsal partner is up to you. But by all means dig in, don't let another opportunity to step on stage and make music pass you by. Here are 10 songs guaranteed to hit the mark – have fun!

WEEKEND WARRIORS
Set List 2 - Ladies Night:
At Last • Chain of Fools
Dancing In The Streets
Heatwave • I Will Survive
One Way or Another
Respect • We Are Family
When Will I Be Loved?
You're No Good

MMO 7162 Weekend Warriors
Piano/Keyboard
ISBN: 978-1-59615-860-3

MMO 7142 Weekend Warriors
Guitar
ISBN: 978-1-59615-861-0

MMO 7152 Weekend Warriors
Bass
ISBN: 978-1-59615-862-7

MMO 7162 Weekend Warriors
Drummer
ISBN: 978-1-59615-863-4

MMO 7181 Weekend Warriors
Female Vocalist - LADIES NIGHT
ISBN: 978-1-59615-864-1

All Weekend Warriors albums are musically coordinated to allow use with each other when performed by a band.

Music Minus One
Call: **800 669-7464** or **914 592-1188**
www.musicminusone.com

Music Minus One

50 Executive Boulevard
Elmsford, New York 10523-1325
800-669-7464 (US) • 914-592-1188 (International)

www.musicminusone.com
e-mail: info@musicminusone.com

ISBN 1-59615-863-4